Russia Implementation of the WTO Agreement

Table of Contents

Introduction

Russia applied to join the General Agreement on Tariffs and Trade 1947 (GATT) in 1993. In 1994, its GATT Working Party was transformed into a working party on its accession to the World Trade Organization (WTO). During the 18 years of Russia's WTO accession negotiations, it worked to modernize its economy and create a stable business environment. WTO Members, for their part, worked to ensure that Russia's legal regime incorporated the key principles on which the WTO is built: national treatment, most-favored nation (MFN) treatment, transparency, and, more generally, the rule of law.

The *Report of the Working Party on the Accession of the Russian Federation to the World Trade Organization* (WPR) identifies over 500 legal measures (such as international treaties, laws, regulations, decrees, resolutions, and other measures) that Russia adopted, amended or modified in an effort to bring its legal regime governing international trade into conformity with the WTO rules. As a result, by the time Russia became a WTO Member on August 22, 2012, it had in place the legislative framework to achieve compliance with its WTO obligations.

Having laws on the books and rules in place, however, does not guarantee WTO compliance or ensure that U.S. workers and businesses will realize the full benefits of Russia's WTO membership. Russia must implement fully its obligations under the WTO Agreement,[1] including the specific commitments undertaken as part of the terms of its accession to the WTO. That task is not of course achieved in a single event; rather, it is an on-going, everyday effort required of every WTO Member.

This Report was prepared pursuant to section 201(a) of the Russia and Moldova Jackson-Vanik Repeal and Sergei Magnitskiy Rule of Law Accountability Act of 2012 (P.L. 112-208). This provision requires the U.S. Trade Representative not later than one year after the United States extends permanent normal trade relations (PNTR) to the products of Russia, and annually thereafter, to submit a report to the Committee on Finance of the Senate and the Committee on

---

[1]   The "WTO Agreement" comprises the Marrakesh Agreement Establishing the World Trade Organization as well as the Multilateral Trade Agreements annexed to the WTO Agreement.

Ways and Means of the House of Representatives assessing the extent to which Russia is implementing the "WTO Agreement" (including the Agreement on the Application of Sanitary and Phytosanitary Measures and the Agreement on Trade-Related Aspects of Intellectual Property Rights) and the progress Russia has made in acceding to the Information Technology Agreement (ITA) and the Agreement on Government Procurement (GPA). In addition, to the extent that the U.S. Trade Representative believes that Russia is not fully implementing its WTO commitments or not sufficiently progressing to accede to the ITA and the GPA, the Report is to describe the actions the U.S. Trade Representative plans to take to encourage Russia to improve its implementation of its commitments or increase its progress toward acceding, as the case may be.[2]

In preparing this report, the Office of the U.S. Trade Representative (USTR) drew on its experience monitoring of Russia's WTO compliance. USTR also drew on the expertise of colleagues in the Departments of Agriculture, Commerce, Homeland Security, State, and Treasury, among other agencies. In addition, USTR published a notice in the *Federal Register* on August 15, 2013, asking for written comments from the public and held a public hearing before the Trade Policy Staff Committee (TPSC) on September 27, 2013. A list of interested parties who submitted comments is set forth in Appendix 1 and the list of persons who testified before the TPSC is set forth in Appendix 2.

Russia became a Member of the WTO just over a year ago, and, as noted, full implementation is a continuing process. Therefore, this report focuses on implementation of Russia's WTO obligations that were, and are, of the greatest systemic and commercial significance and which are important to the full realization of the opportunities presented to U.S. businesses and workers by Russia's WTO membership.

---

[2]   P.L. 112-208 also requires the U.S. Trade Representative to submit annual reports to the Committee on Finance of the U.S. Senate and the Committee on Ways and Means of the House of Representatives describing the enforcement actions taken by Office of the U.S. Trade Representative (USTR) against Russia to ensure Russia's full compliance with its obligations as a Member of the World Trade Organization (WTO). That Report was submitted to the committees on June 18, 2013. In addition, USTR and the Secretary of State are required to submit annually to the same committees a report that describes the actions the agencies have taken to promote the rule of law in Russia and that discloses the status of any pending petition for espousal filed with the Secretary of State by a U.S. investor in Russia.

Executive Summary

During the 18 years of negotiations on the terms for Russia's accession to the WTO, the United States and other WTO Members worked hard to ensure that by the time Russia became a WTO Member, it had made the necessary changes to its legal regime to be in a position to comply with its WTO obligations. Thus, our focus in the first year of Russia's membership in the WTO has been on how Russia is implementing the new regime. We believe that Russia has taken many important steps to implement all of its WTO commitments in most areas, but at the same time, there are several areas where more progress is needed.

With regard to measures applied at the border, Russia reduced tariffs upon becoming a WTO Member as required, and again one year after accession. Importantly for U.S. exporters of information technology products, Russia completed the process to become a participant in the Information Technology Agreement. In the past year, however, the Eurasian Economic Commission (EEC)[3] introduced some "combined tariffs" (adding a minimum specific duty to *ad valorem* rates), on both agricultural and industrial goods, that warrant monitoring to ensure consistency with Russia's WTO bound rates.

In general, Russia has simplified border procedures, for example by reducing customs fees, eliminating certain licensing requirements for imports and implementing WTO rules on customs valuation. The United States continues to monitor Russia's regulatory regime for importation and distribution of encryption products and alcoholic beverages. In addition, the recent imposition of a safeguard measure on combine harvesters has raised concerns about that measure's consistency with the WTO rules. The United States is also watching Russia's export regulatory regime, especially with regard to ferrous scrap.

Agriculture, and in particular the use of sanitary and phytosanitary (SPS) measures to block U.S. exports, was an area of significant concern during Russia's WTO accession negotiations. While we are not aware of concerns regarding Russia's domestic support to its agriculture industry, questions remain concerning Russia's application of the WTO Agreement on the Application of Sanitary and Phytosanitary Measures (SPS Agreement) as well as Russia's specific commitments

---

[3]   As described below, the EEC is the administrative body of the Customs Union of Russia, Kazakhstan and Belarus.

with regard to its application of SPS measures. Russia's (and the EEC's) actions with regard to the adoption of international standards, development of inspection guidelines, establishment lists, and veterinary certificates, have raised concerns in relation to Russia's SPS commitments.

In addition to obtaining increased market access in Russia for U.S. goods, the United States sought significant market opening commitments in Russia for U.S. services. Upon becoming a WTO Member, Russia committed to substantial market openness in a broad range of services sectors, particularly in service sectors of importance to the United States, including financial services, telecommunications, computer and related services, distribution services, and audio-visual services. Russia also took "horizontal" (cross-cutting) commitments related to its regulatory processes and structure. U.S. officials are not currently aware of any issues with Russia's implementation of its commitments to open its services markets since becoming a WTO Member.

Russia's WTO commitments address not only barriers erected at the border, but also internal policies that can favor domestically produced goods over imports. For example, Article III of the GATT, requiring that Members treat imported goods no less favorably than domestically produced goods, is one of the core tenets of the WTO and radiates throughout the WTO Agreement. Russia's "recycling" fee, introduced shortly after it became a WTO Member, raised concerns about the different treatment accorded to domestically produced motor vehicles as compared to imported vehicles. Concerns have also been raised with regard to Russia's regime for collecting copyright levies on products that can be used to reproduce copyrighted material for personal use as well as Russia's application of value added tax (VAT) on royalties for cinema products. As the result of efforts of the United States and other WTO Members, Russia has amended the recycling fee regime to extend the fee to domestically produced vehicles. We will continue to monitor the implementation of this fee for non-discriminatory application, and the overall level of the fee remains a concern. With respect to Russia's application of its copyright levy system and its collection of VAT on royalties for cinema products, the United States will also monitor Russia's application of these measures for consistency with Russia's WTO commitments.

The level of concern with Russia's implementation of its commitments concerning other internal policies affecting trade depends on the particular area. With regard to the distribution of industrial subsidies and the behavior of its state-owned or -controlled enterprises, U.S. officials are not currently aware of major concerns, but are closely monitoring these areas. In the WPR, Russia committed that producers/distributors of natural gas in Russia would operate consistently with normal commercial considerations to recover their costs and make a profit. However, Russia's efforts in this direction have been uneven, and concerns remain about Russia's pricing of natural gas. On the issue of technical barriers to trade, Russia has generally made a strong effort to meet its notification requirements, but the United States has raised concerns with regard to the establishment and functioning of Russia's TBT single inquiry point. With regard to government procurement, in May 2013, Russia became an observer to the Committee on Government Procurement, a step toward initiating negotiations to become a member of the GPA within four years from its accession to the WTO, consistent with its WTO commitment.

The protection of intellectual property rights (IPR) in Russia has traditionally been a key concern of U.S. trade policy. Prior to becoming a WTO Member, Russia amended its IPR laws to integrate WTO requirements into its legal regime. It made numerous changes to its Civil and Criminal Codes as well as other legislation, including customs legislation, in order to improve its regime for protecting and enforcing IPR, including with respect to key rights relied on by the U.S. copyright-based industries. As Russian IPR legislation continues to evolve, the United States will remain engaged to ensure Russia implements fully its WTO commitments. Russia's record with regard to enforcement, however, is weak. The United States has concerns about the use of *ex officio* authority by customs officials at the CU border, the system of collective management of rights, and the protection of IPR on the Internet. The United States-Russian Federation Intellectual Property Right Working Group provides a forum through which the United States will continue to engage with Russia on IPR issues, and the IPR Action Plan, signed by the United States and Russia in December 2012, provides a roadmap of the issues to be addressed.

The WTO's Agreement on Trade Related Investment Measures (TRIMS) seeks to prohibit trade distortive investment requirements, such as those that require the use of domestically produced goods or link a firm's allowable imports to its exports. Notwithstanding Russia's good work toward eliminating TRIMS-inconsistent measures prior to accession, just before the end of the negotiations, Russia expanded its automotive investment incentive programs, which contained certain problematic features. In one of the very few transition periods permitted in the WPR, these programs were allowed to continue until July 1, 2018. The United States will monitor Russia's steps to bring these programs into compliance with the WTO rules by that date and monitor Russia's other investment regimes to ensure their compliance with the TRIMS Agreement.

Much emphasis has been placed on bringing Russia into the rules-based system of the WTO. Knowing what the rules are, being able to rely on the applicability of those rules, and having the means to enforce the rules combine to create a stable environment in which trade can flow. The terms of Russia's WTO accession underscore and strengthen all of those elements. Through its accession negotiations, and in its first year as a Member, Russia has not only notified numerous measures to the WTO, but has embedded into its (and the CU's) legal regime the requirement to publish new measures affecting international trade and to provide interested parties an opportunity to comment. That said, the United States is aware of some areas in which Russia has not met its notification commitments, and will continue to remind Russia of its transparency obligations.

In the coming year, in order to ensure that U.S. businesses and workers realize the full benefits of Russia's WTO membership, USTR, working with other U.S. government agencies, as well as with other WTO Members, will continue to monitor closely Russia's implementation of its WTO commitments. As noted in USTR's Enforcement Report, if Russia or the CU adopts or implements measures that appear not to be consistent with Russia's scheduled commitments -- for example, by restricting market access, imposing discriminatory rules on U.S. exports of goods or services, failing to meet its transparency requirements, or other actions -- USTR will investigate and use all appropriate means to resolve the matter. These means include, as needed, the full panoply of WTO tools, including dispute settlement where appropriate, to ensure that Russia's and the CU's measures (including how they are applied) conform to Russia's WTO obligations. Finally, the ability of USTR to effectively monitor and enforce Russia's implementation of their WTO commitments is affected by resource constraints.

Russia in the World Trade Organization (WTO)

On August 22, 2012, following 18 years of negotiations with the United States and other Members of the WTO, Russia became a Member of the WTO. At that time, however, the United States and Russia each invoked non-application of the WTO Agreement with respect to the other. On December 21, 2012, following the termination of the application of the Jackson-Vanik amendment to Russia and the extension of PNTR to the products of Russia, the United States and Russia both filed letters with the WTO withdrawing their notices of non-application and consenting to have the WTO Agreement apply between them.

Russia and the Customs Union

Russia began its move toward closer economic ties with its neighbors Belarus, Kazakhstan, Kyrgyzstan and Tajikistan by signing the Treaty on the Establishment of the Eurasian Economic Community (EurAsEC) on October 10, 2000.[4] The purpose of EurAsEC was to promote mutual trade and investment on the basis of fundamental principles and norms of international law, including WTO rules, and also to explore the creation of a free trade area and potentially a customs union.[5]

On January 1, 2010, Russia, Kazakhstan and Belarus began implementing a Customs Union (the Customs Union or CU) by adopting a common external tariff (CET). On July 1, 2010, a common CU Customs Code entered into effect, and on July 1, 2011, the CU Parties abolished all customs posts on their internal borders, allowing for the free flow of most goods among the CU Parties. As of July 1, 2010, the CU Commission was responsible for the adoption of CU sanitary and phytosantiary (SPS) technical regulations and other SPS documents.

Beginning in early 2012, the Eurasian Economic Commission (EEC) replaced the CU Commission as the supranational body charged with implementing external trade policy for the CU Parties. When Russia joined the CU, it transferred authority over many aspects of its foreign trade regime to the CU, including import tariff levels, trade in transit rules, nontariff import measures (e.g., tariff-rate quotas, import licensing, and trade remedy procedures), customs

---

[4] Uzbekistan's membership in the EurAsEC was suspended in 2008.
[5] See paragraph 1434 of Russia's WPR.

policies (e.g., customs valuation, customs fees, and country of origin determinations), border enforcement of intellectual property rights, establishment and administration of special economic and industrial zones, and the development of technical regulations and SPS measures. As a result, many of Russia's WTO commitments are implemented through CU measures. In such cases, Russia's WTO commitments specifically provide that they apply whether the Russian government or the competent bodies of the CU are responsible for implementation of the relevant commitment.

Moreover, on May 19, 2011, the CU Parties adopted the "Treaty on the Functioning of the Customs Union in The Framework of the Multilateral Trading System of 19 May 2011" (Treaty on the Multilateral System). According to this treaty, the provisions of the WTO Agreement, as set-out in any CU Party's (e.g., Russia's) Protocol of Accession and WPR, which fell within the competence of the CU, became an integral part of the legal framework of the CU. As such, these provisions were part of the single undertaking and were CU Agreements that were part of the single undertaking for each CU Party. Under the Treaty on the Multilateral System, CU Parties were obligated when making an international treaty in the framework of the CU to ensure that the CU agreement was consistent with the WTO commitments of each CU Party. Similarly, when CU bodies adopted and applied CU acts, those acts had to comply with those commitments. Finally, the CU Parties were required to adopt measures to adjust the CU and decisions of CU bodies to comply with the WTO Agreement as set out in the Protocol of Accession and WPR of each Party. Until those measures were adopted, other CU treaties and decisions of CU bodies would apply only to the extent that they complied with the WTO Agreement. Thus, the rights and obligations of a CU Party under the WTO Agreement would override prior and future CU agreements and decisions of CU bodies.

Import Regulation

Tariffs & Border fees

As a result of bilateral goods market access negotiations with the United States and 54 other WTO Members, Russia agreed to bind all 11,170 tariff lines in Russia's Goods Schedule. Russia's average final bound rate for industrial goods is approximately 7 percent, a decrease from the applied average tariff rate of 10 percent at the time of accession. According to the

WTO, the average final bound rate for agricultural goods will be 10.8 percent, compared to the applied average tariff rate of 13.2 percent at the time of accession.[6] Approximately 38 percent of Russia's tariff lines had their final bound rates implemented upon accession and over 80 percent will have their final bound rates implemented within 3 years of accession. Russia cannot raise the CU CET above these tariff bindings, bringing a large degree of predictability to businesses exporting to Russia.[7]

In the process of binding its tariffs as part of its WTO accession, Russia reduced many tariffs in sectors important to U.S. exporters. For example, Russia agreed to bind its tariffs on wide body aircraft at 7.5 percent; Russia's previously applied tariffs on these products were as high as 20 percent. Russia also committed to an average final bound tariff for plastics of 6.2 percent; Russia previously applied an average tariff of 10 percent. Russia agreed to an average final bound tariff rate of 6 percent on steel products; previously Russia applied an average tariff rate of 8.9 percent. Significantly, Russia agreed to final bound rates on chemical products that are generally consistent with the rates specified under the Chemical Tariff Harmonization Agreement, resulting in an average final bound rate of 5.3 percent. Previously, Russian tariffs on chemicals averaged 6.7 percent and ranged as high as 20 percent.

In the agriculture sector, Russia committed to a final bound tariff of 12.5 percent within 4 years for wine; previously Russia applied a tariff of 20 percent. For pears and other fresh fruit, Russia committed to a final bound tariff of 5 percent, in contrast to its previous applied tariff rate of 10 percent. As a result of the United States' efforts to expand access to Russia's market to U.S. meat products, Russia now applies zero tariffs on pork products imported within the tariff rate quota (TRQ); Russia's previously applied tariff on these products was 15 percent. Likewise, Russia expanded the access to its beef market from 41,700 tons to 60,000 tons through a U.S. country-specific TRQ, with a 15 percent in-quota tariff. In addition, Russia has established access for High Quality Beef with a 15 percent tariff outside of the TRQ for beef. Finally, Russia has committed to a final bound tariff of 5 percent for live animals, with some tariff lines

---

[6] Because of the difficulty in calculating average tariff rates for agriculture products due to the presence of combined tariffs (e.g., x% but not less y rubles per piece), USTR does not calculate a single average tariff for all agriculture products, but we have provided the WTO's data for context.

[7] Because Russia, Kazakhstan and Belarus apply a common external tariff, Russia's WTO tariff schedule effectively binds the CU CET, with some temporary exceptions for Kazakhstan.

at zero percent. Russia previously applied up to a 40 percent tariff on live animals. These tariff reductions, and others, have improved market access for U.S. exports. For example, aerospace sector, U.S. exports to Russia increased by 34 percent from 2012 to 2013, while U.S. metal exports increased by more than 33 percent during the same period. In addition, U.S. consumer goods exports to Russia increased by 20 percent from 2012 to 2013, while U.S. metal exports increased by more than 17 percent during the same period.[8]

A significant aspect of Russia's WTO accession was its commitment to take the steps necessary to join the Information Technology Agreement (ITA), which requires the elimination of tariffs on computers, semiconductors and other information technology products within five years. Upon accession to the WTO, Russia submitted an initial draft ITA schedule that failed to include a small number of important products. The United States and other WTO Members insisted that Russia file a comprehensive and complete ITA Schedule. On September 2, 2013, Russia filed with the WTO Secretariat a revised ITA Schedule with the missing lines included. Following review and approval by members of the ITA committee, on September 13, 2013, Russia became the 78th participant of the ITA Committee. Despite Russia's delay in formally joining the ITA, its commitment to eliminate tariffs on ITA goods was enshrined in its WTO goods schedule from the date of its WTO accession and Russia began implementing the tariff-elimination requirements of ITA membership from the date it became a WTO Member.[9]

Despite its many market opening tariff reductions, Russia's implementation of some of its tariff commitments has raised some concerns. The EEC (the CU body responsible for administering the CU CET) appears to have changed the type of duty on certain lines by augmenting the *ad valorem* rates with an additional minimum specific duty (thereby creating a "combined tariff"). Under WTO rules, the resulting combined tariff must not exceed Russia's bound tariff commitments. In addition, Russia has not informed WTO Members whether, for those goods subject to a combined tariff, the *ad valorem* equivalent of the specific duty is within the WTO *ad valorem* bound duty rate. The United States is carefully monitoring these tariff lines and the

---

[8]   The periods of comparison were January 2012 – October 2012 and January 2013 (immediately following the extension of PNTR) – October 2013 because data for 2013 are available only through October.

[9]   See, section 201(a)(1)(B)(i) of the Act.

United States will work with Russia to ensure that the application of the CU CET does not result in implemented tariffs exceeding Russia's WTO bound rates.

Customs Fees

Upon becoming a WTO Member, Russia agreed to comply with Article VIII of the General Agreement on Tariffs and Trade (GATT) 1994, which requires that fees and charges imposed at the border (other than tariffs) be limited to the approximate cost of the service provided. In fact, Russia specifically committed to amend its system of customs clearance fees in order to reduce those fees, and to establish fixed fees for customs clearance of goods using electronic format or other simplified procedures for filing customs declarations.

Russia's implementation of these commitments is reflected in Article 72 of the CU Customs Code which limits the amount of customs fees to the approximate cost of the service rendered. In addition, Russia revised its fee schedule for customs clearance fees in conformity with its WTO commitments, including providing a lower rate when goods are declared electronically.

U.S. officials are not currently aware of any issues with Russia's implementation of these commitments since becoming a WTO Member.

Customs Valuation

The WTO Agreement on the Implementation of GATT Article VII (also known as the Customs Valuation Agreement or CVA) is designed to ensure that determinations of the customs value for the application of duty rates to imported goods are conducted in a neutral and uniform manner, precluding the use of arbitrary or fictitious customs values. Adherence to the CVA is an important issue for U.S. exporters, particularly to ensure that market access opportunities provided through tariff reductions are not negated by unwarranted and unreasonable "uplifts" in the customs value of goods to which tariffs are applied. Russia agreed to implement its obligations under the CVA, including the interpretative notes, upon accession to the WTO, without any transition period. In addition, Russia took a specific commitment in the WPR not to use reference prices or fixed valuation schedules as a means for determining customs value as well as the right to appeal decisions that were based on a minimum value, fixed valuation schedule or reference price.

Russia (and its CU partners) integrated the basic provisions of the CVA into the CU legal framework. Specifically, the hierarchy of the six methods of customs valuation in the CVA, as well as most, but not all, of the provisions of the interpretative notes, are reflected in Russia's domestic law and implemented by reference in the CU Customs Code.

On occasion, importers have raised concerns that Russia's Federal Customs Service's (FCS) is continuing to use reference prices and is requesting additional documents beyond those normally submitted with an entry to substantiate the importers' declared value (e.g., the shippers export declaration). The United States has encouraged affected parties to challenge inappropriate valuations through the Russian legal system, and, where appropriate, has raised these concerns directly with the FCS. In addition, the United States engages in an ongoing dialogue with the FCS on valuation methodologies in an effort to address the FCS' concerns about under-invoicing, primarily from other countries. The United States will continue to monitor Russia's valuation practices and work with the FCS to ensure full implementation of Russia's commitments on customs valuation.

Trading Rights

The right to import and export (e.g., to declare goods at the border for import and meet relevant requirements, such as payment of any customs duties, SPS measures, technical standards and protection of intellectual property rights (IPR)) without having to invest in the importing country or employ a customs broker to facilitate market access, is very important, especially for small and medium-sized enterprises that may not be able to afford to establish an office in each market or that for commercial reasons need to be the importer of record for the goods. In 1991, Russia eliminated its State monopoly on foreign trade, but prior to its WTO accession, Russia had not only limited the right to import and export goods to Russian enterprises, but also required an "activity license" to engage in the business of importing or exporting (in addition to requiring import licenses on select products). As part of its WTO accession commitments, Russia eliminated the requirement for an activity license to import and export goods. Following Russia's accession, the only requirement to engage in the business of importing and exporting is registration in Russia, and Russia has committed to employing an expeditious and transparent registration policy.

While an activity license is still required as a precondition for obtaining an import license for some products (e.g., alcohol, encryption products and pharmaceuticals), following accession, the importer of record (declarant) is permitted to pay the relevant customs duties, fees and charges in connection with the importation of the goods, and meet other import requirements, but is not required to present an import license. The person withdrawing the goods from the customs checkpoint for distribution in Russia is now responsible for presenting the requisite import and/or activity license.

U.S. officials are not currently aware of any issues with Russia's implementation of these commitments since becoming a WTO Member.

Import Licensing

The Agreement on Import Licensing Procedures (Import Licensing Agreement) establishes rules for all WTO Members that use import licensing procedures requiring the submission of an application or other documentation (other than that required for customs purposes) to the relevant administrative body as a prior condition for importation into the customs territory of the importing Member. The Agreement's aim is to ensure that the procedures used by Members in operating their import licensing systems do not, in themselves, form barriers to trade. An important objective of the Import Licensing Agreement is to increase transparency and predictability and to establish disciplines to protect the importer against unreasonable requirements or delays associated with the licensing regime.

To implement the rules of the Import Licensing Agreement, Russia amended aspects of its import licensing regime to liberalize and simplify the process of importing certain products subject to import control. For example, Russia agreed to eliminate the non-automatic import license requirement for sugar. In addition, when Russia became a WTO Member it eliminated its non-automatic import licensing requirements for spirits and alcohol products and replaced them with an automatic licensing requirement.

Russia also agreed to liberalize its import licensing regime for products with cryptographic capabilities (encryption products). Prior to 2010, Russian law provided that any encryption product required an import license, and that the receipt of an import license was predicated on receiving an import permit from the Federal Security Services (FSB). In the WPR, Russia agreed to establish three categories of encryption goods with corresponding levels of control: 1) encryption goods that can be imported with no customs formalities related to encryption; 2) encryption goods that require only a one-time notification; and 3) encryption goods that require an "import permission" and an import license. In addition, although an activity license to distribute encryption products would be required to obtain an import license for encryption products, a distribution activity license would not be required to import encryption products in the first two categories. Russia also committed to integrate certain procedural safeguards into its licensing regime for encryption products, such as confirming that source code would not be required to obtain an import license and that once an import permission was obtained for an encryption good, the same good or a good used for the same purpose with identical encryption could be imported under an automatic license.

On December 31, 2009, the CU implemented an import licensing regime for encryption products, reducing the procedural hurdles for importing encryption goods into Russia. However, certain aspects of the regime raise concerns with regard to Russia's commitments in this area. For example, the list of products subject to notification does not accurately reflect the definition of products to which Russia agreed in the WPR. Furthermore, in response to U.S. concerns regarding the establishment of a category of encryption goods that can be imported with "no customs formalities," Russia has asserted that a "notification" is not a customs formality and that the rules governing the importation of encryption products are more liberal than they were prior to WTO accession. In addition, U.S. electronics exporters have noted import licenses have, on occasion, been limited to individual shipments, rather than issued for all shipments of the "product family."

Although Russia eliminated the general requirement for an activity license to import and export and shifted to an automatic import licensing regime for alcoholic beverages, it has retained the requirement that an importer have an activity license to produce, warehouse or distribute alcohol in order to obtain a license to import alcoholic products and to purchase the required excise stamps. Alcohol distributors have raised concerns about Russia's seemingly onerous and arbitrary requirements to obtain a warehousing license issued by Russia's Federal Service for Regulation of the Alcohol Market's (FSR) governing the technical condition for storage of alcoholic beverages.

The United States continues to press the Russian government, and the FSB in particular, to address U.S. concerns regarding Russia's implementation of its commitments on import licensing of encryption goods. U.S. officials regularly encourage the FSB to provide greater transparency as well as to engage in frequent dialogue with the private sector. The United States will also continue to work to ensure that alcohol warehouse licensing provisions are transparent and not unnecessarily burdensome.

Non-tariff Measures

During Russia's WTO accession negotiations, there was significant discussion about Russia's regulation of alcoholic beverages. As part of the terms for its accession, Russia agreed to apply its regulatory regime for alcohol products in a non-discriminatory manner, consistent with WTO rules. In particular, Russia committed to ensure that bank guarantees (meant to cover import duties, VAT and excise taxes) would not significantly exceed the total amount of fees actually due. Russia also agreed to apply its excise stamp regime consistent with WTO rules.

To implement these WTO commitments, Russia amended its laws to make all domestic alcohol producers and importers subject to the same reporting requirements for excise stamps on alcoholic beverages. As a result, Russia now requires importers and domestic manufacturers to report their use of excise stamps at the same level of detail,, thereby eliminating the differential treatment applied prior to accession. Russia also eliminated the double guarantee on imported alcohol products which had existed prior to accession.

Although Russia eliminated its domestic provisions requiring double bank guarantees, the CU has established its own bank guarantee requirement to demonstrate full payment of taxes and tariffs. The CU rules appear to allow FCS to accept Russia-specific bank guarantees as evidence of full payment of the CU guarantee. Some Russian customs posts, however, have interpreted these CU rules to require both the CU bank guarantee as well as the Russian bank guarantee. In addition, Russia's FCS often requires bank guarantees far in excess of the actual tax liability of the covered goods. Russian law permits FCS to set the bank guarantee at the highest amount that could be due if the actual amount due cannot be calculated. Industry claims that the information is available that FCS could use to calculate a more accurate (and usually lower) bank guarantee amount. The United States will continue to monitor Russia's regulation of the alcohol market to ensure that its customs control measures are consistent with its WTO commitments.

Trade Remedies

Binding tariffs, and applying them equally to all trading partners, are key WTO principles that contribute to the efficient flow of trade in goods. The WTO Agreement, however, permits certain exceptions to these requirements. Trade remedy measures comprise three such circumstances: 1) actions taken to remedy the effect of imports of goods that are sold below normal value and are causing or threatening to cause material injury ("anti-dumping duties"), 2) actions taken to offset subsidies on imports that are causing or threaten to cause material injury ("countervailing" duties), and 3) measures that address an increase in imports that is causing or threatening to cause serious injury to a domestic industry ("safeguard measures"). Russia committed that, as of the date it became a Member of the WTO, any trade remedy measure in place or any trade remedy measure investigation launched before the date of accession, would be consistent with the relevant WTO agreements on trade remedies, namely the Agreement on Implementation of Article VI of the GATT 1994, the Agreement on Subsidies and Countervailing Measures and the Agreement on Safeguards.

At the time of its accession, Russia was in the midst of transitioning from a Russia-based trade remedy regime to a CU-based trade remedy regime. During the transition period, national regulations governing trade remedy investigations applied to the extent that they did not conflict with the CU regime, but the final decision to impose, extend, review or terminate a measure would be taken by the CU Commission. The CU regime was based on several agreements adopted to implement the WTO requirements on the use of trade remedy laws. Upon the expiration of the transition period on August 1, 2012, national regulations were abolished.

Importantly, Russia made a commitment that any trade remedy investigation or measure would be consistent with its WTO commitments regardless of whether the investigation had been commenced by, or the measure had been put in place by Russia's investigating authority or the CU. To implement these commitments, prior to becoming a WTO Member, Russia revised its trade remedy law (covering anti-dumping, countervailing duty and safeguard measures). The new law established the procedural requirements of the WTO agreements, including for the disclosure of findings and reasoned conclusions on pertinent issues of fact and law, the determination of the accuracy of the information submitted by domestic and foreign parties, and the rights of interested parties to submit comments during the investigation. In addition, the CU Parties adopted several agreements to implement the WTO requirements on the use of trade remedy laws.

When Russia joined the WTO, it notified its trade remedy laws and procedures as required under the transparency provisions of the WTO Agreement and the WPR. It also notified those safeguard investigations that were in process when it joined the WTO, as well as those initiated after it joined the WTO. As to the investigations initiated after it became a Member progressed, Russia met most of its notification requirements, such as providing notifications before taking a provisional measure (including the opportunity to consult with interested parties) and notifications of a decision to apply a final safeguard measure. However, Russia has failed to notify two safeguard measures that are currently being enforced. These measures involve investigations completed prior to Russia becoming a WTO Member and involve caramel and corrosion-resistant pipe and tube. The United States has asked Russia to notify these measures to the WTO.

Although the EEC appears to have met many of the procedural requirements of the WTO Agreement on Safeguards, the EEC's final affirmative safeguards determination, and decision of June 25, 2013, recommending a safeguard measure in the form of an additional tariff of 26.7 percent on imports of combine harvesters, raises concerns in relation to the substantive provisions of the WTO Agreement on Safeguards. For example, the EEC preliminary and final determinations do not appear to address adequately issues relating to causation and serious injury, including data irregularities and omitted data. In addition, in terms of remedy, the EEC introduced a progressive liberalization rate of 0.5 percent over the duration of the safeguard measure (i.e., three years), without any explanation of how the 0.5 percent liberalized rate remedies the serious injury being caused.

The United States, along with the European Union (EU), held several rounds of consultations concerning the proposed safeguard measure. While the EEC noted the substantive concerns raised by both countries, the final determination to impose measures was sent to the Supreme Council of the Customs Union for consideration because of concerns raised by Kazakhstan. On

17

October 15, 2013, the EEC imposed a quota on imported combine harvesters, from January 1, 2014 to August 21, 2016. The United States will continue to monitor the EEC's administration of its trade remedy laws, and in particular, Russia's implementation of the recent safeguard measure on combine harvesters.

Export Regulation

Russia agreed in the WPR to reduce or eliminate export duties on a large number of products, including ferrous scrap (an important steel input) and copper cathode, and bound the tariff level on the remaining products on which it applied export tariffs. Russia also took on the obligations of Article XI of the GATT 1994, which generally prohibits WTO Members from maintaining export restraints (other than duties, taxes or other charges) except those that can be justified under the provisions of the WTO Agreement. Consistent with that commitment, and the relevant CU agreements, Russia eliminated an export ban on grain imposed in 2010. Russia also confirmed that any export restraints imposed to ensure essential materials to domestic producers would not operate to increase the exports of or the protection of that processing industry.

The United States has concerns with respect to the conformity of Russia's and the CU's export licensing provisions with WTO disciplines, and Russia has recognized that work still needs to be done in this area. Russia has amended its national regulations to replace the export licensing regime for precious stones, diamonds and metals with an automatic licensing regime, to reduce the number of goods subject to export licensing, and to remove export bans and other quantitative restrictions on the export of certain types of goods. In addition, Russia has eliminated restrictions on the export of raw materials for pharmaceuticals and reduced the number of pharmaceuticals subject to export licensing. Also, consistent with its specific WTO commitments on ferrous scrap and copper cathode, Russia has reduced its export duties on those products as scheduled in the WPR. Finally, the Russian Ministry of Energy has proposed legislation to liberalize rules governing which Russian companies may export liquefied natural gas, while maintaining Gazprom's current monopoly for Russia's natural gas exports via pipeline to neighboring countries and Europe. The United States continues to monitor the evolution of the Russian and CU export regulatory regime to ensure its consistency with the WTO Agreement.

In 2012, Russia briefly closed some ports in the Russian Far East (RFE) to exports of ferrous scrap and published a notice of intent to close other ports, including St. Petersburg, the largest Russian port for scrap exports. Following a legal challenge in the domestic courts, as well as significant international pressure (including from the United States), Russia reopened the ports in the RFE. Currently, there are no port closures in effect for ferrous scrap and Russian officials have confirmed that the proposed intent to close ports in the Russian northwest has been rescinded. The United States continues to monitor the situation to ensure that Russia does not impose quantitative and other export restraints that would effectively negate Russia's commitment to reduce export duties on ferrous scrap.

Agriculture

Upon its accession to the WTO, Russia assumed the obligations of the WTO Agreement on the Application of Sanitary and Phytosanitary Measures (SPS Agreement) as well as the WTO Agreement on Agriculture, which contains commitments in three main policy areas for agricultural products -- market access, domestic support and export subsidies. Russia also made a number of additional agriculture-related concessions on its level of financial support for agricultural production, as specified in the WPR.

Sanitary and Phytosanitary Measures

The SPS Agreement explicitly recognizes the right of WTO Members to take certain measures necessary to protect human, animal, or plant life or health. However, the SPS Agreement requires Members to avoid arbitrary or unjustifiable distinctions in the levels of protection in different situations if such distinctions result in discrimination against a good from another WTO Member or constitute a disguised restriction on international trade.

Under the SPS Agreement, each Member is free to determine its own appropriate level of SPS protection. Once a WTO Member has established its appropriate level of protection, the SPS Agreement provides that the SPS measures it takes to achieve that level of protection must be based on scientific principles, must not be maintained without sufficient scientific evidence, and may be applied only to the extent necessary to protect human, animal, or plant life or health. The SPS Agreement also requires each Member to ensure that its SPS measures are based on an assessment, as appropriate to the circumstances, of the risk that a particular substance or product, including a process or distribution method, poses to human, animal, or plant life or health.

Russia assumed these obligations, and specifically committed to ensure that all of its SPS measures, whether adopted by it or the competent bodies of the CU, would be based on international standards, guidelines and recommendations unless a more stringent measure is justified by a risk assessment. Russia further committed that measures which were not based on international standards, guidelines or recommendations would not be applied in Russia without providing Members a scientifically-based justification of the measures, in accordance with the SPS Agreement. Russia also specifically confirmed that all SPS measures, whether adopted by Russia or by the competent bodies of the CU, would comply with the non-discrimination provisions of the SPS Agreement. SPS measures would not, Russia agreed, be used in such a way as to constitute a disguised restriction on international trade.

In addition to assuming these general commitments under the SPS Agreement, Russia undertook specific obligations in the WPR, for example: to negotiate and sign veterinary certificates that comply with World Organization for Animal Health (OIE) requirements for Bovine Spongiform Encephalopathy attestations; to base its requirements for goods subject to veterinary control on international standards; to ensure that its measures do not discriminate between imports from WTO Members or between Russia's products and imports; to accept international standards regarding certain antibiotic residues; and to ensure that any actions that are taken in response to non-compliance with Russian or CU requirements are proportional to the non-compliance.

Russia confirmed the criteria for "de-listing" an establishment (an action which has the effect of prohibiting imports from that establishment), and in particular, committed to notify the exporting Member and give the exporting Member time to propose corrective measures. With regard to emergency measures, Russia confirmed that its decisions and procedures for de-listing would be in accordance with the WTO SPS Agreement. Russia further confirmed that, by the time of accession, specific inspection guidelines would be developed that reflected the principles of equivalence and that were based on international standards, guidelines and recommendations. Russia also agreed to remove certain veterinary control measures, such as establishment approval for selected products, and confirmed that veterinary control measures applied to animal products would only be modified in accordance with the SPS Agreement.

To ensure compliance with the WTO rules on transparency, Russia confirmed that all Russian normative legal acts relating to SPS measures would be published in Russia's two official journals and that CU Commission (and EEC) Decisions and CU legal acts relating to SPS measures would be published on the CU website. Russia further committed that drafts of SPS technical regulations and other mandatory requirements would be made publicly available for comment and that interested persons would have at least 60 days to provide comments on the drafts. Finally, Russia has established an SPS inquiry point and established a website with full detailed conditions for import of specific products.

Because the authority over many SPS matters was transferred to the CU, most of the measures necessary to implement Russia's WTO SPS commitments must be adopted at the CU level. However, Russia's national SPS measures continue to apply to the extent that they do not conflict with CU measures.

In order to assure WTO Members that Russia would implement its commitments regarding harmonization with the international standards, recommendations, and guidelines, Russia, and the CU, amended existing legislation and adopted new measures. The CU adopted decisions that committed Russia to three key principles: in the absence of CU or Russian requirements, the relevant international standards would apply; if there are stricter CU or Russian requirements that lack scientific justification, the international standards would apply; and lastly, that Russia and/or the CU would align its standards with the relevant international standards or provide a scientific justification following a request from an interested party, including foreign governments. In addition, Russia established a process for reviewing those SPS measures that interested parties believe are inconsistent with the international standards. Through this process, interested persons can request that specific SPS measures that are inconsistent with international standards be brought into conformity with the relevant international standard.

By 2011, the CU had established common veterinary requirements and 40 common forms of veterinary certificates for imports into the CU territory from any third country. The United States and other Members expressed concern that many of the common veterinary requirements appear to be more stringent than the relevant international standards and did not allow the conditions in an exporting country to be taken into account. To allow exporting countries the opportunity to address these concerns with regard to some of the requirements in the common veterinary certificates, the CU Commission extended the validity of bilateral veterinary certificates and provided Russian officials with the authority to negotiate certificates with exporting countries with terms that differ from CU common requirements. In addition, the CU Commission confirmed the CU Parties' right to amend the CU certificates and requirements to reflect international standards established by the OIE and Codex Alimentarius (Codex), allowing the United States to negotiate bilateral certificates with the CU Parties that may differ from the CU common form, and which reflect better the conditions of trade between the United States and Russia.

The United States and other WTO Members also expressed concern regarding the veterinary requirements adopted by the CU, which included a requirement that all veterinary controlled products must come from an establishment approved by the CU Parties. In order to address concerns regarding the extension of this requirement to many products, including lower risk products, the CU Commission removed the establishment requirement for certain products including dairy and pet food upon Russia's accession.

To implement Russia's commitments with regard to inspections, the CU Commission established the basis for joint inspections, systems audits and acceptance of exporting country's guarantees. In addition, Russia committed to adopt inspection guidelines reflecting the principles of equivalence and the relevant international standards and confirmed that it would not suspend imports from establishments based on the results of on-site inspections before it had given the exporting country the opportunity to propose corrective measures. To implement Articles 4 and 5 of the SPS Agreement concerning equivalence and risk assessment, the CU Commission established the basis for determining equivalence and conducting risk assessments in accordance with international standards.

Although Russia has put in place the legal framework to allow it to comply with its WTO commitments, its implementation of these commitments remains problematic. On many fronts, Russia does not appear to have implemented fully its commitments to apply international standards, or, where it applies a more stringent standard, to provide a science-based, objective risk assessment. Moreover, in those cases where Russia has provided the United States with a risk assessment purporting to justify its SPS measures, those assessments do not appear to have been conducted taking into account risk assessment techniques of relevant international organizations. For example, Russia has adopted a zero tolerance for ractopamine, a standard more stringent than Codex's maximum residue levels (MRL) for pork and beef but does not appear to have provided a risk assessment that conforms to Codex guidelines. In addition, Russia has a near zero tolerance for tetracycline residues, a standard more stringent than Codex's MRL, but again appears to have failed to provide WTO Members with a risk assessment that conforms to international guidelines. We continue to raise our concerns about Russia's risk assessments both bilaterally and in the WTO.

Russia committed to develop guidelines for inspections of meat processing and storage facilities, fish and fish products, and dairy and dairy products in accordance with the relevant international standards. Although the CU Commission issued the requisite decision, the necessary guidelines are still under development. USTR and the U.S. Department of Agriculture (USDA) are working with Russia to ensure that the guidelines are in line with the international standards.

Related to the inspections issue is the difficulty of obtaining Russia's acceptance of an exporting country's guarantees for approving establishments. Notwithstanding Russia's commitments regarding inspections and establishment approvals described above, acceptance of guarantees and approval of establishments has become more difficult. In many cases, Russia has taken many months before issuing approvals or, in some cases, Russia has refused, without any apparent reason, to approve a facility until after an on-site inspection has been conducted by the CU Member State veterinary services. The United States continues to raise this issue with Russia bilaterally and with Kazakhstan.

The United States is also concerned with Russia's implementation of obligations to remove certain veterinary control measures for lower risk products. In 2011, the CU adopted a decision removing such veterinary controls. However, days before Russia became a WTO Member, Russia's veterinary service proposed a temporary measure that would maintain the establishment requirement for all veterinary products until after a successful audit has been completed. Despite strong objections by the United States and other WTO Members, Russia is still implementing this requirement. The United States has raised this issue bilaterally with Russia on the margins of the SPS committee and continues to strongly encourage Russia to address U.S. concerns regarding Russia's implementation of the CU decision and its compliance with its obligations to remove certain veterinary controls.

In order to meet its WTO commitments, Russia agreed to negotiate veterinary certificates with the United States that differ from the CU certificates after receiving United States' substantiated requests. Because the United States' current bilateral certificates remain valid, U.S. officials have focused on those products, such as dairy, where the United States does not currently have access to the Russian market. However, Russia and its CU partners insist on including attestations in the certificates that are not based on international standards, notwithstanding Russia's commitments to conform its attestations to such standards. Engagement on new certificates has been difficult, with inconsistent participation by the CU Parties' experts and a lack of coordination among the CU Parties. For example, after 15 months and engagement by U.S. senior officials, we received feedback on a U.S. proposed dairy certificate. The initial feedback did not reflect a coordinated CU position, but following insistence from the United States, the CU Parties provided a coordinated response. In addition to continuing to work through multiple fora to engage on certificate negotiations, USTR and USDA continue to work with Russia and Kazakhstan to improve the engagement in this area.

Domestic Supports and Export Subsidies

When Russia joined the WTO, it was still restructuring its agriculture sector to recover from decades of central planning and an imbalance in prices and revenue. To support development and employment in the rural territories, and to encourage agricultural production, Russia had in place numerous subsidies. Nevertheless, Russia committed to a $9 billion aggregate measure of support (AMS) binding for 2012 and 2013, which is a short-term increase over its current trade-distorting spending. Importantly, however, Russia has committed to phase down its domestic agriculture support payments to $4.4 billion by 2018, a level below its spending level at the time of accession. Moreover, Russia has accepted an obligation to ensure that the sum of all product-specific support does not exceed 30 percent of the non-product specific support. Finally, Russia agreed to eliminate all of its export subsidies. U.S. officials are not currently aware of any issues with Russia's implementation of regarding agricultural subsidies since it became a WTO Member.

Value-Added Tax

To further level the playing field between imported agriculture products and domestically-produced agriculture products, Russia agreed to eliminate the exemption from VAT payments for certain domestic agriculture products. The United States is monitoring Russia's implementation of this commitment.

Services

The General Agreement on Trade in Services (GATS) provides a legal framework for addressing barriers affecting trade and investment in services. WTO Members assume obligations under the GATS to provide market access, national treatment, MFN, and other obligations; in addition, the GATS provides a forum for further negotiations to open services markets around the world. These commitments are contained in a Member's services schedule, just as a Member's tariff commitments are set out in a schedule.

In its services schedule, Russia committed to substantial openness in a broad range of services sectors, including through the elimination of many existing limitations, particularly in service sectors of importance to the United States, such as financial services, telecommunications, distribution, energy, express delivery, professional services and audio-visual services.

Russia also took "horizontal" (cross-cutting) commitments related to its regulatory processes and structure. During the years of Russia's WTO accession negotiations, it undertook a series of steps to improve the business environment in Russia, including streamlining the processes for company registration and reducing the number of activities subject to licensing. To address concerns of WTO Members about its activity licensing regime, Russia committed to making publicly available the measures affecting trade in services, as well as the names of the competent authorities responsible for issuing licenses. Russia undertook specific commitments to ensure transparency in the process for granting (and denying) licenses and to ensure that the relevant regulatory authority would not be accountable to any service provider it regulated in sectors where Russia had taken specific commitments. Russia further committed to instituting notice-and-comment requirements to ensure transparency in the development of the regulatory regime governing those same sectors. Russia's services commitments also establish the rules for business visas for executives and professionals, and allow service companies to transfer vital employees to their operations in Russia.

Financial services

Russia undertook significant market opening commitments in the financial services sector, including allowing 100 percent foreign ownership of all commercially meaningful types of non-insurance financial services firms, including banks, broker dealers, and investment companies. Russia agreed that foreign companies can own and trade the full range of securities (including state securities, bullion and new instruments once they are approved), lead-manage Russian securities issuance, and participate in financing of privatization of government-owned firms. Russia has also agreed to allow important cross-border services such as financial leasing, financial information, and data processing, as well as credit cards and other types of payments.

With regard to insurance, Russia has agreed to provide a significant level of market access and national treatment for U.S. insurance companies, including 100 percent foreign ownership of non-life insurance firms. Russia has also committed to phase out its existing restrictions on foreign insurance firms. Limits on the number of life insurance licenses granted to foreign insurance firms, as well as foreign participation in a small number of mandatory insurance lines, will be phased out over 5 years. Russia will allow foreign insurance companies to open direct branches for life and non-life insurance, reinsurance, and services auxiliary to insurance nine years from the date of its accession.

Telecommunications

Russia agreed to open its market for telecommunication services, both on a facilities and non-facilities basis, to all WTO suppliers as of the date of its accession to the WTO. Sectoral coverage is comprehensive and Russia will allow telecommunications companies to operate as 100 percent foreign-owned enterprises. Importantly, Russia eliminated the requirement that a fixed satellite operator must establish a commercial presence in Russia in order to provide capacity to a Russian telecommunications company. Russia also accepted the pro-competitive WTO Basic Telecommunications Reference Paper that requires the establishment of an independent regulator, the prevention of anti-competitive behaviour by dominant suppliers, and the introduction of transparency obligations and interconnection requirements.

Computer and Related Services

Russia committed to not limit market access and to extend national treatment to all computer and related services, including on a cross-border basis. This latter commitment is particularly valuable, given the growth of cloud computing, which is covered by Russia's WTO commitments. An ongoing challenge is how this commitment will be implemented in light of Russia's 2001 Data Protection law, which includes an "adequacy" standard to ensure privacy protection of the data similar to that in the EU, but has yet to provide alternative mechanisms to allow for the transfer of personal information outside of Russia without the consent of the data subject. The United States will monitor Russia's implementation of this commitment.

Distribution Services

Russia committed to liberalize its wholesale, retail and franchise sectors, by allowing foreign distributors to operate as 100 percent foreign-owned enterprises upon its accession to the WTO. U.S. distributors will be allowed to engage in the distribution of most products, including nutritional supplements, with minimal limitations and on terms comparable to those of domestic distributors. In addition, Russia's WTO commitments for distribution provide for direct sales by individual commission agents. However, rules that require that sales of specialized dietary products containing biologically active substances be sold only through pharmacies and specialized stores remain in effect. These restrictions may raise questions with regard to Russia's compliance with its commitment to allow direct sales of such products. The United States will urge Russia to revise these measures in order to clarify the legal status of such sales.

Audio-Visual Services

Russia made strong commitments in its dynamic audio-visual sector, including in motion picture distribution and projection services, and the sale of programming to television and radio stations. Russia has also agreed to allow foreign audio-visual companies to operate as 100 percent foreign-owned enterprises.

U.S. officials are not currently aware of any issues with Russia's implementation of its WTO GATS commitments since it became a WTO Member, but will continue to monitor Russia's implementation of its services commitments.

Internal policies affecting trade

Non-discrimination

In its WPR, Russia agreed to assume the obligations of GATT 1994, the WTO agreement that establishes the core principles that constrain and guide WTO Members' policies relating to trade in goods. Two core principles of the GATT are the Most-Favored Nation (MFN), or non-discrimination, rule – referred to in the United States as "normal trade relations" – and the rule of national treatment.

The MFN rule for goods (set forth in Article I of GATT 1994) attempts to put the goods of an importing WTO Member's trading partners on equal terms with one another by requiring the same treatment be applied to goods of any origin. Article I of GATT 1994 generally provides that if a WTO Member grants one WTO Member's goods a benefit or advantage, it must immediately and unconditionally grant the same benefit or advantage to like goods imported from all WTO Members. This rule applies to customs duties and charges of any kind imposed in connection with importing and exporting. The rule also applies to internal taxes and charges, among other internal measures. The MFN rule with regard to services (set forth in Article II of the General Agreement on Trade in Services (GATS)) imposes comparable obligations, but only with respect to services that have been scheduled by each WTO Member.

The national treatment rule with respect to goods (set forth in Article III of GATT 1994) complements the MFN rule. It is designed to put the goods of an importing WTO Member's trading partners on equal terms with the importing Member's own goods by requiring, among other things, that a WTO Member accord no less favorable treatment to imported goods than it does for like domestic goods. Generally, once imported goods have crossed the national border and import duties have been paid, the importing WTO Member may not subject those goods to internal taxes or charges in excess of those applied to like domestic goods. Similarly, with regard to measures affecting the internal sale, purchase, transportation, distribution or use of goods, the importing WTO Member may not treat imported goods less favorably than like domestic goods.

The national treatment rule applies in a similar manner to services under Article XVII of the GATS. This provision requires a WTO Member, in sectors in which it has taken commitments in its schedule, to accord no less favorable treatment to services and service suppliers of other WTO Members than it accords to its own like services and service suppliers.

Russia's WPR elaborates on Russia's commitment to apply both Articles I and III of GATT 1994, as well as Article II of GATS. Throughout the 18 years of accession negotiations, Russia reviewed its laws and regulations and made an effort to revise those that conflicted with its WTO MFN and national treatment obligations, e.g., regarding prices charged for railway transport, application of internal taxes, subsidies for new automobiles, and the right to import and export. In addition, Russia, in conjunction with its CU partners, reviewed the CU agreements, regulations and decisions to ensure their conformity with the MFN and national treatment provisions of the WTO Agreement.

However, national treatment concerns have been raised in connection with the imposition of a number of Russian measures and policies. Soon after it became a WTO Member, Russia adopted a "recycling" fee on motor vehicles, purportedly to cover the cost of recycling the vehicle at the end of the vehicle's life and to develop a recycling industry in Russia. Domestic producers, however, were exempt from paying the fee on domestically-produced vehicles if they agreed to assume the cost of recycling the vehicle at the end of its life. Vehicles imported from Kazakhstan and Belarus were also exempted from paying the fee. The United States, as well as other WTO Members, raised concerns about the potentially WTO-inconsistent nature of this program. The EU and Japan sought consultations with Russia regarding this fee under the WTO dispute settlement mechanism, and the United States participated in both of those consultations. On October 10, 2013, the EU requested the establishment of a WTO dispute settlement panel. Shortly thereafter, Russian President Putin signed a law extending the recycling fee to domestic automobile manufacturers, regardless of any producer's commitment to recycle its vehicles. Some concerns remain, however, concerning the overall level and calculation of the fee. Vehicles imported from Kazakhstan and Belarus are also now subject to the recycling fee. The United States will monitor the implementation of the new law to ensure its compliance with Russia's WTO commitments.

National treatment concerns have also been raised in connection with Russia's copyright levy system. Russia collects a levy on both domestically-produced and imported products that can be used to reproduce copyrighted material for personal use (e.g., video recorders, voice-recorders, photocopy machines, etc.) However, the list of domestically produced products on which the levies are paid appears to differ from the list of imported products on which the levies are paid. In addition, the reporting and payment systems also appear to differ. FCS provides information on imports to the Ministry of Culture, which in turn provides the information to the collecting society to verify the payment of the levies, whereas domestic manufacturers pay based on sales, and self-notify. U.S. officials have raised concerns regarding these practices with Russia and will continue to work to address these concerns.

The United States also has concerns regarding national treatment with regard to taxation of royalties on motion pictures. Russia applies an 18 percent VAT on payments for "right to use" (i.e., licensing royalties) cinema products. However, the recipient of the royalty can apply for a VAT rebate if the cinema product is "Russian" (defined as movies with a Russian producer; majority of authors are Russian residents; at least 30 percent of the cast and crew are Russian residents; the movie is in the Russian language; at least 50 percent of the movie is financed by Russian residents; or the film is produced under special international agreements). In other words, the VAT collected on royalties paid to show a "Russian movie" (as defined in the Russian Tax Code) can be reimbursed whereas the VAT paid on royalties to screen a U.S. (or other non-Russian) movie cannot be reimbursed. This practice raises concerns about Russia's implementation of its national treatment commitments. The United States will work to ensure that Russia collects VAT on royalties consistent with its WTO commitments.

Industrial Policy, Including subsidies

Upon its accession to the WTO, Russia assumed obligations under the WTO Agreement on Subsidies and Countervailing Measures (SCM), which addresses the use of countervailing duty measures by WTO Members. In the WPR, Russia committed that it would eliminate, by the time of its accession, all subsidy programs prohibited under Article 3 of the SCM, i.e., subsidies contingent on export performance (export subsidies) and subsidies contingent on the use of domestic over imported goods (import substitution subsidies). In addition, Russia took a specific commitment to extend subsidies to foreign-made aircraft for the purchase or lease of aircraft that had previously been available only for the purchase or lease of Russian-made aircraft.

With regard to its transparency commitments, both during its accession negotiations and as a Member, Russia provided subsidy notifications to the WTO Committee on Subsidies and Countervailing Measures (Subsidies Committee). The United States has raised questions about the comprehensiveness of those filings, and requested additional information with respect to several other programs which Russia has not notified.

During Russia's WTO accession negotiations, Members raised concerns about specific subsidy programs related to automobiles, civil aircraft and agricultural equipment. Russia has eliminated its "cash for clunkers" program, which offered vouchers toward a new Russian-built car to people who turned in a car more than 10 years old; and in the civil aircraft industry, Russia terminated the program which limited subsidies to only Russian-made planes (although a few existing contracts were grandfathered). In an effort to bring its railroad tariffs (rates) for grain into compliance with its WTO commitments, Russia amended its preferential railroad tariffs, effective on September 3, 2013. Under the new program, these tariffs are not region or direction specific, and hence can apply to any grain moving in any direction, provided the distance is greater than 2,000km. In practice, however, these subsidies (a reduction in the railroad tariff of 67 percent) may benefit only Siberian grain because of the 2,000km minimum distance requirement. In addition, with regard to agricultural equipment, questions remain about the WTO consistency of the program under which Russia disburses financial support to producers of agriculture equipment which may be contingent on a certain level of local production.

Concerns have also been raised with respect to certain benefits provided to manufacturers in the "Titanium Valley" SEZ. According to industry sources, the primary beneficiary of these programs is Verkhne Saldinskoye Metallurical Production Association (VSMPO), currently the only titanium producer in Russia. VMSPO exports 70 percent of the titanium it produces. Russia has not notified its Titanium Valley SEZ programs to the WTO Subsidies Committee. Another possible subsidy to the titanium industry (i.e., VSMPO) may have occurred in the form of the allegedly below-market price paid by Norcom in its purchase of VSMPO from the Russian Government.

The Russian government has in place a variety of initiatives aimed at supporting various domestic industries, with particular focus on agriculture and agriculture equipment. The United

States will continue to examine Russia's subsidy notifications and to monitor Russia's subsidy policies and programs, with particular attention to the aviation industry as well as the agriculture and agricultural equipment industry, to ensure Russia implements its commitments under the SCM.

State-owned or –controlled Enterprises

In addition to the disciplines on the activities of state-owned and state-controlled enterprises in the WTO Agreement, Russia also agreed to some further disciplines in the WPR. In particular, Russia agreed that state-owned and state-controlled enterprises, when engaged in commercial activity, would make purchases, which were not intended for governmental use, and sales in international trade in a manner consistent with the WTO Agreement. Such enterprises would make purchases and sales of goods and services in accordance with commercial considerations, such as price, quality, marketability and availability, and afford enterprises of other WTO Members the opportunity to compete for participation in such purchases and sales. These commitments covered all goods, as well as services covered under Russia's Schedule of Specific Commitments, taking into account the limitations set out in its schedule, the rights and obligations of Russia under the GATS, and recognizing the regulatory measures of Russia covered by the WTO Agreement.

As confirmed in the WPR, Russia has many state-owned enterprises and state-controlled enterprises that operate in the commercial sphere. Prior to becoming a WTO Member, Russia took various steps to eliminate special privileges for most of those companies. For example, in 2002, Russia abolished the exclusive right of Alrosa, or any other exporter, in the activities of diamond production and export. In 2005, Russia abolished the law under which only certain companies in which the government owned no less than 51 percent were allowed to import or export ethyl spirit (provided they had the appropriate license). Similarly, in 2009, Russia abolished the exclusive rights of Almazyuvelir Export Foreign Trade Association with respect to operations in raw materials containing platinum and platinum group metals.

One industry with state involvement that raised concerns during Russia's WTO accession negotiations was the civil aircraft industry. As discussed above, Russia agreed to eliminate its WTO-inconsistent subsidies for the aircraft industry. In addition, during its WTO accession negotiations, Russia confirmed that its majority ownership in Aeroflot, the national airline, would not accord it undue influence in that company's commercial activity. In the oil and gas sector, the only company with an exclusive right to export gas at the time of Russia's accession was the state-owned company Gazprom, which controlled all exports of natural gas from Russia. However, Russia is considering proposals to allow other companies to export liquefied natural gas, while retaining Gazprom's monopoly of pipeline gas exports. U.S. officials are not currently aware of any issues with Russia's implementation of these commitments since becoming a WTO Member, but the United States will monitor these industries to ensure that Russia implements its WTO commitments.

Pricing Policies

In the WPR, Russia agreed that it would not use price controls to restrict the level of imports of goods or services, or for the purpose of protecting the production of domestic goods or impair its services commitments. In addition, Russia listed in the WPR the limited number of products and services remaining subject to price control or government guidance pricing, and it provided detailed information on the procedures used for establishing prices.

Russia also specifically committed to unify the rail transportation charges (separate from the subsidies to rail transportation of grain described above) to ensure that, by July 1, 2013, products imported into, and products destined for exportation or sold for export from, Russia would face the same transportation charges. Russia further committed that regulated railway tariffs would be published before they entered into force. In December 2012, Russia's Federal Tariff Service issued an order governing its tariff policy on rail freight and published draft measures and orders on its website.

With regard to natural gas, Russia was allowed under its WTO commitments to continue its domestic price regulatory regime. Russia committed that producers/distributors of natural gas in Russia (including Gazprom, but also so-called independent producers Rosneft and Novatek) would operate -- within the relevant regulatory framework -- consistent with normal commercial considerations to recover their costs and make a profit. However, Russia's progress in meeting this commitment appears to be modest and uneven. In 2007, Russia started a long-term process to equalize the return on domestic gas sales as compared to the return on international gas sales.

However, Russia has continued to delay the date by which Russia will achieve equal profitability of export and domestic industrial sales, including through a rate ("tariff") freeze for domestic utility consumers adopted in September 2013. As a result, it appears that the domestic price for industrial users may be below export prices. The United States will continue to monitor the pricing of natural gas in the Russian market.

Standards, Technical Regulations and Conformity Assessments

As a WTO Member, Russia has assumed the obligations of the Agreement on Technical Barriers to Trade (TBT Agreement), which establishes rules and procedures regarding the development, adoption and application of standards, technical regulations and the conformity assessment procedures (such as testing or certification) used to determine whether a particular product meets such standards or regulations. The TBT Agreement's aim is to prevent the use of technical requirements as unnecessary barriers to trade. The TBT Agreement applies to all products, including industrial and agricultural products. It establishes rules that help to distinguish legitimate standards-related from protectionist standards-related measures. The TBT Agreement requires, among other things, that standards-related measures are to be developed and applied transparently and on a non-discriminatory basis by WTO Members and shall be based on relevant international standards and guidelines, when appropriate.

Russia's standards-related measures are implemented through EEC and CU measures as well as through Russian domestic requirements. In the WPR, Russia committed to comply with all provisions of the TBT Agreement, including those relating to transparency and predictability. In addition, Russia has taken specific commitments with regard to technical regulations affecting the telecommunications equipment and civil aviation sectors.

As a new WTO Member, Russia is taking action to comply with the TBT Agreement's transparency obligations by notifying to the WTO proposed technical regulations, but a fully transparent, standardized system for providing notifications on TBT issues is not yet in place in Russia. In the WPR, and through its required notifications (particularly that under Art. 15.2 of the TBT Agreement), Russia pledged to use a single "inquiry point". Russia's TBT inquiry point procedure, however, appears to be deficient because its functions are split between two different government ministries, leading to confusion and inadequate transparency. The United States will continue to encourage Russia to create a single TBT inquiry point in order to establish a regularized, comprehensive notification system consistent with the TBT transparency requirements.

Although Russia has notified many technical regulations to the WTO, those notifications appear to be less than comprehensive. Russia appears to be taking a narrow view regarding the types of measures that need to be notified. For example, Russia has not notified its new registration requirements for alcohol products. It has also failed to notify amendments made to its Federal Law on Circulation of Medicines, a draft law, decree and registration procedures concerning medical devices, and various other legislative acts establishing technical standards, regulations governing the required installation of GLONASS-compatible navigational systems in civil aircraft as well as revisions to amendments to the EEC's regulations governing food labeling published in October 2012. To comply fully with the WTO's transparency requirements for technical regulations and conformity assessment procedures, Russia must notify to the WTO all regulations and conformity assessment procedures that meet the notification requirements of the WTO, and ensure that interested persons have adequate time to submit comments and to have those comments taken into account.

Regulation of Russia's alcoholic beverage sector has raised a number of concerns about consistency with the substantive requirements of the TBT Agreement. At the national (i.e., Russian government) level, there has been a long-standing requirement to register alcoholic beverage products with Federal Supervisory Service for Protection of Customers Rights and Human Well-Being (Rospotrebnadzor). Effective October 1, 2013, the Russian Federal Service for the Regulation of the Alcohol Market (FSR) introduced new procedures establishing a notification requirement for both existing as well as new-to-market alcoholic beverages sold in the Russian market. Much of the information required by FSR in its notification appears duplicative of information already provided to Rospotrebnadzor in the registration process. Furthermore, FSR provided a transition period of only four months between publication and implementation. (In addition, the EEC is considering yet another level of registration, further duplicating in large part the registration and notification procedures already applied at the national level.) U.S. officials have raised concerns with the Russian government about these duplicative notification measures and the short timeframes for implementation (as well as the warehouse licensing practices discussed above), and have requested that Russia notify these measures to the WTO. Some of these new regulations may not be consistent with international standards and may be more burdensome than necessary. The United States will continue to work with Russia to ensure its alcohol control regime is consistent with its WTO commitments.

The possibility of duplicative requirements has also arisen in the toy industry where conformity certifications or declarations of conformity for toys from non-CU accredited laboratories are apparently not accepted. As a result, toys must undergo duplicative testing procedures. Moreover, elements of the CU regulation "On Safety of Toys" may not be based on international standards.

Another sector in which the regulatory regime has raised concerns is food labeling. Recent amendments to the EEC's regulations on food product labeling impose numerous labeling requirements. Among other concerns, the revised regulations appears to require labeling for genetically engineered products, allergens and nutritional components beyond the recommended guidelines established in the Codex General Standard for Food Labeling. In addition, the revisions appear to require that products containing sweeteners carry warning statements that may not to be based on the latest scientific research and may not be consistent with Codex.

The United States has raised transparency concerns (failure to notify and inadequate comment opportunity) both in meetings of the WTO Committee on Technical Barriers to Trade as well as in bilateral meetings. Often Russia has followed up by notifying the regulations in a reasonable period of time. The United States will continue to monitor Russia's technical regulations and work with Russia and the EEC to ensure that these measures meet the requirements of the TBT Agreement. In addition, the United States will continue to remind Russia of its transparency obligations.

Government Procurement

GATT 1994 and the GATS do not cover the purchase of goods and services "for government use" (i.e., government procurement). The rules governing international trade in government procurement are instead found in the WTO Agreement on Government Procurement (GPA), a plurilateral agreement which currently includes 43 WTO Members (including the United States). The GPA applies to government procurement of goods and services, and requires GPA members to provide MFN and national treatment to the goods, services and suppliers of other GPA members and to adhere to detailed procedures designed to ensure fairness, predictability and transparency in the procurement process. At present, Russia is not a GPA member. It committed to request observership in the GPA upon its WTO accession, and in May 2013, it became an observer. Russia also committed to initiating negotiations to become a member of the GPA by tabling an offer within four years from its accession to the WTO.[10]

However, as a WTO Member, Russia is required to adhere to GATT and GATS which provide that purchases of goods and services, including by state-owned or state-controlled enterprises, which were not purchased for governmental purpose, but with a view to commercial resale or for use in the production of goods or services for commercial sale, are not considered government procurement, and hence subject to these provisions. U.S. officials are not currently aware of any issues with Russia's implementation of these commitments since becoming a WTO Member.

Intellectual Property Rights

Upon joining the WTO, Russia assumed all the obligations of the Agreement on Trade-Related Aspects of Intellectual Property Rights (TRIPS Agreement) and the additional commitments on IPR issues contained in the WPR. The TRIPS Agreement sets minimum standards of protection for copyrights and related rights, trademarks, geographical indications, industrial designs, patents, integrated-circuit layout designs and undisclosed information. The TRIPS Agreement also establishes minimum standards for the enforcement of intellectual property rights in administrative and civil actions and, at least in regards to copyright piracy and trademark counterfeiting, in criminal actions and in actions at the border. Furthermore, the TRIPS Agreement requires that, with very limited exceptions, WTO Members provide national and MFN treatment to the nationals of other WTO Members with regards to the protection and enforcement of IPR rights.

In the WPR, Russia undertook additional commitments on IPR protection and enforcement, such as clarifying how undisclosed information and test data will be protected in Russia, withdrawing exceptions to copyright protection for copyrighted works that existed prior to 1994, reviewing

---

[10]   See, section 201(a)(1)(B)(ii) of the Act.

and improving the operation of its collecting society regime, and updating law enforcement procedures to address certain issues related to digital piracy of copyrighted materials.

Legal Framework

Prior to its accession to the WTO, Russia amended its IPR laws to integrate WTO commitments into its legal regime and with the objective of implementing the 2006 United States-Russia bilateral IPR agreement. Russia improved its civil protections for IPR by amending Part IV of its Civil Code, which relates to protection of various forms of IPR, including patents, trademarks, and copyrights and related rights, to update its civil enforcement procedures and adopt the legal framework for Russia's implementation of the World Intellectual Property Organization (WIPO) Internet Treaties. Russia also amended its Civil Code to clarify that an existing domain name would not serve as a ground for refusal to register a third party's trademark or service mark for that name. Russia also standardized its patent fees to apply in the same manner to Russian and non-Russian entities.[11]

In recent years, reflecting commitments in the WPR, Russia has made progress toward implementing controls on unlawful optical media production, notably through amendment of its Law on Activity Licensing, to ensure that copyright infringers cannot renew a license to engage in optical media production. Russia also revoked its reservation to Article 18 of the Berne Convention for the Protection of Literary and Artistic Works. As a result, Russia now provides copyright protections for works that existed prior to 1995 and originated from the United States or any other Party to the Berne Convention or the WTO Agreement.

In the WPR, Russia committed to taking action against operation of websites that promote illegal distribution of content protected by copyright or related rights. In June 2013, Russia approved its first law specifically dedicated to decreasing online piracy of television and film. Legislative measures are currently being drafted to amend the law. The United States will monitor closely evolving laws and practices related to online piracy.

---

[11]   At the time this Report was drafted, Russia was considering further amendments to Part IV of its Civil Code, including with respect to addressing piracy over the Internet. Because Russia's Duma is still considering those proposed amendments, we have not yet fully evaluated them. The United States will, however, remain engaged on this matter.

In the WPR, Russia also committed to ensure that the thresholds for the application of criminal procedures and penalties with regard to cases of willful trademark counterfeiting or copyright piracy on a commercial scale would be set and applied in a manner that reflected the realities of the commercial market place. Accordingly, Russia amended its Criminal Code to establish fines and to reflect adjustments to the threshold for the application of criminal procedures and penalties for willful counterfeiting or commercial-scale piracy. For example, administrative fines for criminal trademark violation had been extremely low. In August 2013, Russia implemented a method of calculating such fines, replacing an arbitrarily low and fixed fine with a fine calculated based on the value of the counterfeits being produced or sold. This method should result in penalties that have a stronger deterrent effect. In addition, as called for in the WPR commitments, Russia ensured that its Civil Code does not predicate protection of a well-known trademark on its inclusion in Russia's List of Well-Known Trademarks.

Russia's customs law also required alteration to strengthen IPR protection. In December 2010, Russia adopted the law "On Customs Regulation" to provide for *ex officio* authority for customs officials and strengthened the *ex officio* provisions contained in the CU Customs Code. The law also updated procedures for registering certain intellectual property rights with the Russian Customs IPR Register. Russia, however, has yet to fully harmonize its IPR regime with the regulatory principles adopted under the CU.

In 2010, Russia passed amendments to the Law on the Circulation of Medicines to protect undisclosed test or other undisclosed data generated to obtain marketing approval for pharmaceutical products, including six years of protection for such data from reliance by subsequent marketing approval applicants for the same pharmaceutical product. These amendments came into force the day Russia became a WTO Member. However, we have yet to see final regulations that include the detailed provisions necessary to ensure implementation of such protection. The United States will continue to monitor this situation closely.

Enforcement

Russia committed, upon becoming a WTO Member, to apply fully the WTO provisions for enforcement of IPR, without recourse to any transitional period. In the WPR, Russia also committed to take "expeditious action" against acts of infringement on the basis of complaints lodged by rightholders and through other means with the objective of eliminating such acts in Russia. Russia made specific commitments to conduct unannounced inspections of plants licensed to produce optical media bearing content protected by copyright or related rights, and Russia continues to conduct such raids. Russia also established a specialized court for intellectual property disputes, which began operating in the summer of 2013, and senior Russian officials have reportedly been working to create a specialized intellectual property agency which would consolidate patent, trademark and copyright matters, including administration of collective management organizations. Such a reform, if executed, would likely not be in place until mid-2014.

Notwithstanding these actions, the current IPR enforcement environment in Russia remains weak. End-user software piracy and sales of counterfeit goods are two particular concerns. Additionally, online piracy has been, and remains, a significant problem in Russia. Russia committed to take enforcement measures against online piracy and to ensure that existing law is applied to prevent certain types of devices or services from circumventing technical protection measures protecting copyrighted content. Russia recently enacted legislation providing a framework to combat certain types of online piracy (as discussed above), and the United States will continue to monitor whether the recent legislative changes and any additional amendments of the law result in taking appropriate action against web sites of the type identified in USTR's Notorious Markets Report.[12]

Furthermore, the information currently available appears to indicate that overall enforcement of IPR has decreased, rather than increased, over the past few years. One ongoing barrier to Russia's adequate and effective enforcement of IPR is the lack of resources devoted to hiring and training law enforcement personnel to investigate and prosecute IPR crimes. Specifically, the number of criminal raids declined significantly in 2012 and the amount of resources devoted to IPR economic crime enforcement has sharply declined over the past two years. Moreover, there has been a notable decline in *ex officio* actions by law enforcement.

---

[12] USTR publishes an annual report on notorious markets as part of its Special 301 review, which identifies examples of prominent physical and online markets in which pirated copyright or counterfeit trademark goods are reportedly available.

Russia's size and geographic location make enforcement of IPR at its borders an essential component of IPR protection. In the WPR, Russia committed that, from the date of its accession, it would encourage its Customs Officials to use their *ex officio* authority to strengthen enforcement against acts of infringement at the border. Russia needs to work with the other CU Parties to ensure that the regulatory principles adopted under the CU principles are executed in a manner that most effectively protects IPR. The United States will continue to monitor Russia's progress in this regard.

Russia's collecting society regime remains nontransparent and burdensome, making it difficult for rightsholders to be fairly compensated for the use of their intellectual property. Although not required under the TRIPS Agreement, Russia committed in the WPR to reviewing its system of collective management of rights and this review appears to be ongoing. Russia also stated that it intended to phase out non-contractual license management within 5 years of Part IV of the Civil Code entering into force. Part IV of the Civil Code entered into force on January 1, 2008, yet Russia has not yet phased out its non-contractual management system. Russia's legislature is considering further amendments to these IPR provisions. The United States will be engaging further on these issues through the United States-Russian Federation Intellectual Property Rights Working Group (IPR WG) and other means.

The United States engages intensively with Russia on a broad spectrum of IPR issues, including TRIPS, through the IPR WG, which is co-chaired by USTR for the United States and the Ministry of Economic Development for Russia. In December 2012, the United States and Russia agreed to an Intellectual Property Rights Action Plan under the auspices of this Working Group. The Plan endorses action to improve a number of IPR priorities, including increased enforcement actions against counterfeit goods, effective prosecution of persons responsible for IPR crimes, establishment of a mechanism for appropriate Internet Service Provider (ISP) liability for copyright infringement, and dedication of resources and personnel to law enforcement agencies to investigate and prosecute online IPR crime. This year, the IPR WG discussed enforcement of intellectual property laws, initiatives to combat the sale of counterfeit pharmaceuticals online, improving procedures in criminal legal proceedings, and other topics of mutual concern. The United States will continue this substantive dialogue with Russia to ensure full implementation of Russia's WTO commitments, IPR Action Plan and all other IPR matters identified in this Report.

Investment

Trade-Related Investment Measures

The Agreement on Trade-Related Investment Measures (TRIMS Agreement) prohibits trade-related investment measures that violate a Member's obligations under Article III (national treatment) and Article XI (general elimination of quantitative restrictions) of GATT 1994. The TRIMS Agreement thus requires elimination of measures such as those that require or provide benefits for the use of domestically produced goods (local content requirements), or measures that restrict a firm's imports to an amount related to its exports or related to the amount of foreign exchange a firm earns (trade balancing requirements).

During the 18 years it was negotiating its WTO accession, Russia worked to bring its investment-incentive programs into compliance with the TRIMS disciplines. For example, prior to its WTO accession, Russia had in place a law that required production sharing agreements (PSAs) to include obligation to purchase a certain percentage of Russian technical equipment for natural resource extraction and to employ a certain percentage of Russian citizens. In preparation for WTO membership, Russia amended its law governing PSAs to provide that for all PSA contracts signed after Russia's WTO accession any WTO-inconsistent provisions in such contracts would be invalidated or brought into conformity with the WTO Agreement. In addition, Russia has stopped concluding PSA agreements. Similarly, in the aircraft sector, in August 2001, Russia eliminated the exemption from customs duties and taxes for temporary import for aircraft, aircraft parts and engines and simulators which were imported under investment agreements.

In the WPR, Russia agreed that, except for measures subject to a specific transition period, all of its laws, regulations or other measures concerning matters covered in the TRIMs provisions of the WPR, whether adopted by it or the competent bodies of the CU, would be consistent with its WTO commitments, and in particular with the TRIMS Agreement, as of the date of Russia membership in the WTO. WTO Members agreed to provide Russia with a transition period to bring two programs that comprise Russia's automotive assembly investment incentive regime into WTO compliance. The first program, introduced in 2005, allows for the duty-free entry of auto parts used in the production of vehicles that contain a certain level of Russian content. In December 2010, Russia initiated a second automotive industry investment incentive program that increased the production volume significantly and the domestic content requirement to qualify for duty free entry of auto parts. In the WPR, Russia committed to cap the requirement to purchase or use domestically produced parts and components at 25 per cent of the ex-factory price of the automobiles. Russia also agreed to eliminate the elements of both of its investment incentive programs that are inconsistent with TRIMS by July 1, 2018, and to begin consultations in July 2016 with the United States and other WTO Members on WTO-consistent measures it could take in this sector.

Since Russia became a WTO Member, in response to concerns raised by the United States and other Members in the TRIMS Committee, Russia eliminated the program under which the Ministry of Agriculture provided loans to farmers at an interest rate below the market rates for the purchase of farm machinery manufactured in Russia.

Russia continues to promulgate policies to encourage domestic production. For example, Russia's Ministry of Economic Development has established a 15 percent price preference for goods (including pharmaceutical) of Russian or Belarussian origin in purchases for government use. Two additional measures are still in draft form: a draft government resolution limiting state and municipal government purchases from a specified list of medical devices to devices produced in the CU and a draft resolution banning pharmaceutical companies from submitting foreign-made drugs for government tenders if two local producers of the drug are listed on the Russian Registry of Medicines. In 2012, Russia issued a decree requiring that most aviation satellite navigational systems be GLONASS (Global Navigational System – Russia's satellite navigation system) or GLONASS/GPS enabled over the next several years, with foreign manufactured equipment being given two extra years to comply. Similar requirements have been published for most forms of public transport, with plans announced requiring private vehicles to begin using GLONASS features. In early 2013, the Ministry of Trade and Industry issued draft decrees limiting government purchases of cars to cars made in Russia or Belarus.

Because Russia is not a member of the Government Procurement Agreement, its local content requirements for government purchases may not implicate its WTO commitments. Nevertheless, the United States has sought, and will continue to seek, information on these programs bilaterally and in the appropriate WTO fora to ensure Russia's compliance with its commitments under the TRIMS Agreement. In addition, the United States is monitoring Russia's implementation of its automotive industry investment programs for compliance with its WTO commitments and will work with Russia to bring its automotive industry investment incentive program into conformity with its WTO obligations by July 1, 2018. USTR has already solicited information on steps Russia was taking to eliminate the WTO-inconsistent aspects of the programs.

Special Economic Zones

Upon accession to the WTO, Russia undertook to apply the provisions of the WTO Agreement throughout its territory, including in its special economic zones (SEZs), which were established to encourage investment through the extension of certain incentives. Russia has transition periods to implement this commitment for the Kaliningrad and Magadan SEZs. To implement that commitment, Russia adopted a new law on SEZs which did not impose any export performance or local content requirements on operations in SEZs. In addition, all customs duties, VAT and excise taxes due on goods imported into the SEZs were to be paid when those goods were released into the chain of commerce in Russia whether or not those goods were further processed. Moreover, Russia agreed to apply all CU agreements governing SEZs in a manner consistent with its WTO obligations and to work with its CU partners to amend any CU agreements or regulations to ensure their consistency with Russia's WTO commitments.

Rule of Law

In order to address major concerns raised by WTO Members during its lengthy WTO accession negotiations, Russia committed to broad legal reforms in the areas of transparency, uniform application of laws and judicial review. Implementation of these reforms will strengthen the rule of law in Russia's economy and help to address pre-WTO accession practices that made it difficult for U.S. and other foreign companies to do business and invest in Russia.

EurAsEC/Customs Union

As noted above, Russia transferred authority for many aspects of its trade regime to the CU. The administrative bodies of the CU include the Court of the EurAsEC, which has competence, *inter alia*, over disputes of an economic nature arising from the implementation of decisions of the bodies of the EurAsEC and of the EurAsEC treaties. When the EurAsEC Court was originally created it did not have jurisdiction to opine directly on Russia's WTO commitments nor could it rule on Russia's compliance with those commitments. However, after the Treaty on the Multilateral Trading System was adopted, the EurAsEC Court received the legal authority to provide advisory opinions on whether a CU act violates WTO rules. Furthermore, the right to bring a case to the EurAsEC Court is not limited to the CU parties or the bodies of the CU. Additionally, individuals with a specific interest can also challenge CU acts in the EurAsEC Court.

Transparency

One of the core principles of the WTO Agreement reflected throughout Russia's WPR is transparency. Transparency permits markets to function effectively and reduces opportunities for officials to engage in trade-distorting practices behind closed doors. Many of the constituent WTO agreements contain initial as well as annual notification requirements to ensure that WTO Members are aware of any new measures being implemented and have the opportunity to raise questions and concerns with regard to those measures.

Russia agreed in the WPR to submit all the required initial notifications by the date of its accession, with the exception of five notifications which were to be submitted within specified deadlines following its accession. In addition, Russia committed to establish formal notice and comment procedures for proposed measures pertaining to or affecting trade in goods, services, and intellectual property; to provide WTO Members and interested parties with decisions in writing setting out reasons for the decision; and to institute new rights of appeal of decisions. These obligations apply to measures that the EEC adopts and that are applied in Russia as well as to Russia's domestic laws, regulations and other measures. Russia has also undertaken specific commitments regarding transparency on issues ranging from application of the price controls to fees charged for engaging in importing or exporting goods.

To implement Russia's transparency commitments at the CU level, the CU Commission established the procedures for publication and public comment on proposed CU legal acts, including that draft decisions shall be published no fewer than 45 calendar days before the Commission meeting at which the decision will be considered. The EEC provided additional details concerning sanitary and phytosanitary quarantine and veterinary-sanitary measures, including requiring that draft decisions and recommendations be published for no fewer than 60 calendar days prior to adoption of such measures. This mechanism appears to provide that these CU measures will not become effective prior to their publication.

During the 18 years of its accession negotiations, Russia provided the required initial notifications as part of the WTO review of its trade regime. With regard to the notifications which were due after Russia's date of accession, all but one, concerning its import licensing requirements, have also been provided to the WTO. As described above, Russia has notified many modifications and/or updates to its trade regime (e.g., TBT measures, SPS measures, trade remedy actions, etc.) as required under its transparency commitments. Russia has also implemented its commitment to provide trade data to the WTO's Integrated Data Base.

Pursuant to its WTO commitments, Russia has established an SPS inquiry point where information about its SPS regime can be readily found. As noted above, Russia's TBT inquiry point, however, remains problematic because its functions are split between different government ministries, leading to confusion and inadequate transparency.

Notwithstanding Russia's many notifications, the United States has identified certain measures (e.g., technical regulations and subsidies) which Russia has not notified. Likewise, Russia has not yet fulfilled its commitment under Article 7.3 of the Import Licensing Agreement to respond to the Questionnaire on Import Licensing Procedures. The United States has also identified specific Russian and CU laws, decisions, regulations, resolutions, and other measures that are a part of Russia's import licensing regime that have not yet been notified. Finally, the United States has asked Russia to notify its regional trade arrangements, including the CU, to the WTO.

Judicial Review

The right of appeal to an independent tribunal or judicial review, providing prompt and effective review for economic matters, is a fundamental component of the WTO Agreement and, in fact, is explicitly required in many of the agreements annexed to the WTO Agreement. Russian law appears to ensure the right of appeal on customs-related matters (both actions and inactions), tax issues, the protection of IPR and technical regulations (including SPS issues). Moreover, Russia has specifically committed that it will provide the right for independent review consistent with its WTO commitments.

Because many aspects of Russia's trade regime have been transferred to the CU, Russia has worked, and continues to work, with its CU partners to adopt the legal acts necessary to ensure that WTO Members and their nationals have recourse to the EurAsEC Court which has jurisdiction over CU issues, including whether Russia or the other CU Parties have effectively implemented CU acts related to WTO issues.

U.S. officials are not currently aware of any issues with Russia's implementation of these commitments since becoming a WTO Member.